Original title:
What I Left Behind

Copyright © 2024 Swan Charm
All rights reserved.

Author: Kene Elistrand
ISBN HARDBACK: 978-9916-89-661-7
ISBN PAPERBACK: 978-9916-89-662-4
ISBN EBOOK: 978-9916-89-663-1

Etched in the Sand

Footprints fade with the tide,
Memories leave no trace.
Waves wash over dreams,
Time's delicate embrace.

Beneath the sun's warm glow,
Secrets linger near the shore.
Each grain a story told,
Whispers of days before.

The horizon calls to me,
A journey yet to start.
Yet in this fleeting moment,
I leave you with my heart.

As shadows dance at dusk,
The sky painted in gold.
I cherish every breath,
In this sand, love's hold.

So when you walk this path,
And find my name in the grain,
Remember what we had,
Etched in time, like the rain.

The Fragrance of Farewells

In the air, a scent lingers,
Of roses and of tears.
Goodbyes painted with heartache,
A dance of fleeting years.

Your laughter haunts the silence,
Like echoes from the past.
Every moment cherished,
Yet nothing seems to last.

The soft perfume of yesterdays,
Carries me through the night.
Each whisper brings a memory,
As stars begin to light.

I walk the paths we traveled,
In shadows cast by time.
With every fragrant moment,
I dream of what was mine.

Though distance pulls us apart,
And the world feels so wide,
Your scent will forever linger,
In my heart, you abide.

Wandering Echoes of the Past

Footsteps in the twilight,
Tracing lines of old,
Whispers of forgotten dreams,
Stories waiting to be told.

I roam through fields of visions,
Where shadows softly play.
Each echo brings a memory,
Of a bright, sunlit day.

The laughter of lost voices,
Rings out through the trees.
I pause to catch their secrets,
Carried lightly by the breeze.

Time's gentle hand keeps pulling,
Drawing me back to you.
In every darkened corner,
A glimmering past shines through.

So I'll wander through these echoes,
With a heart still full of grace.
For every pause and heartbeat,
Is a memory I embrace.

Ink Smudges on a Blank Page

In the quiet night, I write,
Thoughts spill like stars so bright.
Words blur and slip away,
Ink smudges on a blank page.

Fingers stained, a subtle trace,
Echoes dance in empty space.
Fragments of dreams come alive,
As shadows from the past thrive.

Hopes and fears in tangled lines,
Captured moments, hidden signs.
In the chaos, clarity grows,
The heart spills what it knows.

Beneath the weight of silence,
In every stroke, a defiance.
Letters weave a tapestry,
A story written just for me.

Yet as the dawn begins to break,
The truth of me, I dare not shake.
With ink smudged, I pen my fate,
On this blank page, I await.

Paths Not Taken

In the forest, shadows play,
Choices linger, lost in gray.
Every step, a turn of fate,
Paths not taken resonate.

Branches reach like whispered words,
Sing of dreams and silent birds.
Wandering hearts in search of light,
Veering off, lost from the sight.

With every choice, a story grows,
Life unwinds where no one goes.
Somber echoes in the night,
Paths not taken, out of sight.

Rivers flow through memories cold,
Tales of courage yet untold.
In the heart, a gentle ache,
Yearning for the roads we make.

But still we tread, our journey clear,
With every moment, drawing near.
In shadows cast, the dreams awaken,
In every heart, paths not taken.

Resonance of Lost Echoes

In the halls of memory's gaze,
Fleeting whispers, faded days.
Echoes linger, softly blend,
Resonance of what won't mend.

Footsteps on a dusted floor,
Time stands still, forevermore.
Voices call from distant past,
In their longing, shadows cast.

Melodies of joy and pain,
Rise like smoke, dance like rain.
Every note, a heartbeat's trace,
Lost echoes in time and space.

Through the cracks where light peeks through,
Fragments of me merge with you.
In the silence, stories bloom,
Resonance fills a vacant room.

Yet in this stillness, I find peace,
In echoes' song, my thoughts release.
For every memory left to know,
A resonance in the ebb and flow.

The Memory Box Gathering Dust

In the attic, a box sits still,
Memories wrapped in faded will.
Each token tells a silent tale,
The memory box gathering dust.

Photographs in sepia hue,
Capture moments, me and you.
Letters bound with fragile string,
Whispers of what the past would bring.

Secrets locked in careful folds,
Stories waiting to be told.
Each trinket holds a little spark,
In shadows cast, we find a mark.

As years roll by, the dust will fade,
Yet in the heart, they still cascade.
Within these walls, the past will hum,
The memory box, forever young.

So I revisit all that's lost,
In every moment, count the cost.
For time may fade, but love will stay,
In the box where memories play.

Remnants of a Shattered Dream

In twilight's grasp, I stand alone,
Fragments scattered, dreams overthrown.
Whispers of hope, now shadows crawl,
Echoes of joy - I've lost it all.

Time's gentle hand, now feels so rough,
What once was bright, now feels too tough.
Memories linger, like smoke in air,
A tapestry torn, beyond repair.

Yet in the ruins, glimmers gleam,
Flickers of light, a forgotten theme.
I gather the shards, piece by piece,
Hoping one day, my soul finds peace.

Ghosts of My Former Self

In the mirror's gaze, a stranger stares,
Faded reflections, burdened cares.
Echoes of laughter, shadows of pain,
Ghosts of the past, in each refrain.

Footsteps whisper on a winding street,
Moments lost, where dreams once meet.
I wander through hallways, dimly lit,
Memories linger, I cannot quit.

Yet still I seek the light of dawn,
To wake the spirit, I thought was gone.
With each heartbeat, I reclaim the thread,
Embrace the ghosts, let them be fed.

Traces of Time's Passage

Softly ticking, the clock unwinds,
Moments slipping, like grains of sand.
A whirlwind rush, a fading glow,
In echoes of laughter, I feel the flow.

Seasons change, the colors fade,
In twilight's grip, foundations laid.
A tapestry woven, each stitch a sigh,
Time's soft whispers, as days go by.

Yet in the stillness, I hear the call,
The essence of life, in rise and fall.
Each second counts, a fleeting gift,
In traces of time, my spirit lifts.

Memories Like Dust

In corners hidden, the dust collects,
Memories linger, the heart reflects.
Fragments of laughter, whispers of tears,
Time's gentle hands, nurturing fears.

Each speck a story, waiting to breathe,
Tales of the past, we weave and believe.
With every sweep, they float and swirl,
Lost in the shadows, a fleeting world.

Yet in my heart, they quietly stay,
Guiding my footsteps, lighting the way.
For even in silence, their echoes remain,
Memories like dust, soft as the rain.

Fractured Reflections

In the mirror, shadows play,
Fragments of a fading day.
Glances stolen from the past,
Whispers of a love to last.

Shattered pieces on the ground,
Silent echoes all around.
Faces blur, their time erased,
Within the glass, a heart displaced.

Dreams long lost, they flutter near,
Haunting visions, crystal clear.
Each likeness tells a different tale,
A haunting wind, a soft exhale.

In the stillness, truth will break,
A path of light that we must take.
Time will heal, though cracks remain,
In every fracture, love's refrain.

The Weight of Unpacked Wishes

Beneath the stars, desires bloom,
Each wish unfurling in the gloom.
Heavy hearts in search of flight,
Curled up dreams, lost in the night.

Silent prayers, a fragile thread,
Hopes untold, they fill the spread.
Laden thoughts, they break and bend,
As moments rush, they never end.

The weight is felt, yet seldom shared,
In quiet corners, souls laid bare.
Each yearning tugs, a tender hand,
Guiding us to solid land.

In shadows cast, we chase the glow,
A fervent spark, an inward flow.
Unpacked wishes, rise and soar,
On wings of faith, forevermore.

A Heart Adrift

Lost at sea, the heart will roam,
Drifting far from hearth and home.
Waves of doubt and currents strong,
Yearning for where I belong.

Castaway thoughts, they rattle deep,
In restless tides that steal my sleep.
An anchor tossed, too far from shore,
In silent cries, I seek for more.

Stars above, my guiding light,
A compass forged in darkest night.
A mapless journey, paths untold,
I'll find the shores, brave and bold.

With every swell, I dance anew,
Embracing waves, I break through blue.
A heart adrift, yet bound to feel,
In every tide, love's gentle reel.

Lanterns on a Stormy Night

Flickering lights in tempest's roar,
Guiding souls to safety's shore.
Each lantern glows, a beacon bright,
In the dark of stormy night.

Raindrops dance on cobblestone,
Murmurs echo, whispers drone.
But through the chaos, hope remains,
A warmth that breaks the raging chains.

Beneath the skies of charcoal gray,
Beacons shimmer, lead the way.
Hearts unite with every glance,
In stormy weather, we find chance.

Through the howling winds, we stand,
With open hearts and outstretched hands.
Lanterns rise above the fray,
Lighting paths for a brighter day.

The Relics We Held Dear

In boxes hidden, dust now clings,
Faded photographs of what joy brings.
Threads of laughter stitched in time,
Woven memories set to rhyme.

Familiar scents of days gone by,
Echoes of love that dared to fly.
Whispers of stories softly fade,
In the twilight, dreams are laid.

Each trinket tells a tale untold,
A legacy of love so bold.
Through fragile moments, we descend,
To find the heart that will not end.

Shining gems of moments past,
Bridges built to make them last.
Grains of sands in an hourglass,
Life's reminders that often pass.

Relics cherished, time stands still,
In every heart, a quiet thrill.
We hold them close, though days grow near,
In every tear, the love is clear.

Footsteps Disappearing in Time

The path we walked, now overgrown,
Fading traces of seeds we've sown.
Echoes linger, calling me back,
To where our laughter filled the crack.

In twilight's glow, shadows extend,
The road once bright seems to bend.
Every step tells a story rare,
Of dreams once shared, now stripped bare.

Time's river flows, relentless tide,
Leaving footprints that slowly hide.
With every breath, a memory fades,
Lost in the fabric that time parades.

But in the silent whispers at night,
I find the warmth of fading light.
Those footsteps, though gone from view,
Still lead me back, to me and you.

Walking through the echoes of days,
Where sunlight danced in golden rays.
Though paths may part, and time may chime,
We'll meet again, as dreams align.

Shadows of Unfinished Chapters

In the margins of our shared tale,
Words unsaid, like ships that sail.
Stories linger, like shadows cast,
In the quiet of nights that pass.

Ink of memories stains the page,
Frozen moments of love and rage.
Fragments woven, strands of gold,
In silent whispers, secrets told.

Each chapter ends, yet lingers here,
In every doubt, in every fear.
The ink we spilled, both bright and dark,
Shadows dance around the spark.

Pages turn in the book of life,
Joy entwined with whispers of strife.
But unfinished, our tale remains,
In twilight's glow, where love sustains.

Oh, let us write a brand new start,
With every beat of a faithful heart.
In shadows that forever leap,
New stories born in valleys deep.

Verses of a Lost Connection

In tangled webs of words unspoken,
Silence hangs where hearts were broken.
Once we danced to a tender beat,
Now only echoes find their seat.

Messages sent on the winds of fate,
Drifting softly, we hesitate.
Chasing dreams that seemed so near,
Only to find them drowned in fear.

The rhythm falters, notes collide,
In empty spaces where we confide.
What once was vibrant, fades to gray,
As distance creeps and hearts decay.

In the twilight glow of what we sought,
Verses linger, though love's forgot.
A melody once pure and true,
Now a haunting, a ghost of you.

Yet in the silence, hope may bloom,
In shadows cast by love's own room.
We'll write again, though paths diverge,
For in lost lines, our hearts emerge.

Reflections in the Still Water

In quiet pools the skies are caught,
The world above, in silence, thought.
Each ripple whispers tales of old,
Of fleeting moments, brave and bold.

Beneath the surface, secrets hide,
Time's gentle flow, a soothing guide.
In crystal depths, I see my face,
A fleeting glance of time and space.

The trees lean close, their branches sway,
To hear the waters softly play.
Echoes dance on tranquil seams,
Carrying the weight of dreams.

As twilight falls, the colors fade,
The world transformed, yet unafraid.
Each wave reflects a story's thread,
Of things I've done, and words unsaid.

In stillness, wisdom shows its worth,
The vast expanse, the quiet earth.
In every drop, a tale unfolds,
A memory, a heart that holds.

Tokens of a Time Gone By

Once cherished, now they fade away,
Old photographs of yesterday.
Faded smiles and laughter's grace,
Hold hints of love in time's embrace.

Fragments of a life once lived,
In every token, hope must give.
Letters yellowed, words sincere,
Ink like memories, crystal clear.

The fragrance of an old perfume,
Reminds me of a sheaf in bloom.
Coins and trinkets, stories swell,
In whispers of a wishing well.

A dusty box beneath the stairs,
Holds echoes of our childhood dares.
Each treasure marked with joy and pain,
A bittersweet remembrance chain.

Tokens linger, but time moves fast,
The shadows of our past are cast.
Yet in my heart these things remain,
The pieces of life's sweet refrain.

Shadows Clinging to Memories

Faded echoes in the night,
Whispers soft, a dimming light.
Shadows dance in rooms once bright,
Memories held, yet out of sight.

Faces linger in the gloom,
Silhouettes in every room.
Time has cast its heavy shroud,
While silence forms a matted crowd.

The ticking clock, it marks the pain,
Each steady beat, a soft refrain.
Moments trapped in twilight's hold,
Stories waiting to be told.

In every corner, tales unfold,
Of dreams once chased, and wishes bold.
Yet shadows cling, reluctant to flee,
As echoes yearn to still be free.

Through the darkness, sparks of light,
Guide me softly through the night.
For every shadow has its grace,
In the memories we embrace.

The Journey of Untraveled Roads

Paths unknown lie in the mist,
A call to adventure, I can't resist.
With every step, my heart does race,
As dreams and fears interlace.

The map is blank, yet hope is clear,
A journey forged, both far and near.
With open arms, I greet the new,
Discovering the dusk and dew.

Winding trails through ancient woods,
Lead me to unknown neighborhoods.
Where every bend brings fresh delight,
And takes me closer to the light.

Mountains high and valleys deep,
Whispers of the earth I keep.
Each road I take, a lesson learned,
In flames of passion brightly burned.

Though paths may twist and turn away,
I walk with courage, come what may.
For in each step, my spirit grows,
Embracing all those untraveled roads.

Unwritten Scores of Our Lives

In silence we compose the notes,
Each moment a new measure floats.
With dreams as ink, we write the line,
A symphony that feels divine.

A pause, a breath, the tempo slows,
Our hearts beat soft in gentle prose.
Each journey takes a different tone,
In harmony, we sing alone.

The chorus echoes through the night,
With whispers of forgotten light.
A melody of hopes and fears,
Together, played through all the years.

In hidden staves, our secrets lie,
Unsung refrains beneath the sky.
Each note a tale of love and strife,
Unwritten scores of our own life.

So let us dance to what we find,
The music born from heart and mind.
For in this song, we all take part,
The unwritten scores that shape our heart.

The Stories Buried in the Earth

Beneath the soil, the ancients lie,
Their whispers mingled with the sky.
Roots unearth tales of olden days,
In nature's grasp, the past displays.

The stones remember every sigh,
Echoes of lives that passed them by.
Footprints fade, but memories stay,
The stories buried, come what may.

In silence, secrets take their place,
Histories woven in time and space.
Under the surface, truth resides,
In every layer, life abides.

The wind carries fragments of lore,
Echoes of those who came before.
In every seed, a tale is sown,
The stories buried, now our own.

Let us remember what was there,
In gentle soil, the past lays bare.
With open hearts, we dig and dream,
Discovering life's fragile seam.

The Sound of Closure

In twilight's hush, a peace descends,
The final notes of a song that ends.
A gentle sigh, the curtain falls,
In silence, life's deep echo calls.

With every end, a chance to start,
We carry on with open heart.
The sound of closure speaks so clear,
Bringing comfort, calming fear.

A chapter closed, yet wisdom gained,
In fleeting moments, nothing's drained.
For every loss, a lesson learned,
In soft goodbyes, our souls have turned.

The waves recede, the shore embraces,
New paths evolve in quiet spaces.
In echoes of what was once known,
The sound of closure, softly grown.

So let this be our final song,
A symphony where we belong.
In every ending, life renews,
The sound of closure, sweet and true.

Forgotten Faces in the Mirror

Reflections dance in twilight's glow,
Forgotten faces, long ago.
With every glance, a story fades,
In silent whispers, memory wades.

The lines of time etch deep and wide,
In mirrors' gaze, we try to hide.
Yet truth remains in every sigh,
Forgotten faces, passing by.

Each wrinkle holds a memory dear,
A fleeting glimpse of yesteryear.
In fogged glass, we search in vain,
For faces lost, yet not in pain.

We age like seasons, come and go,
Collecting echoes from the flow.
In every glance, we seek to find,
Forgotten faces, intertwined.

So let us cherish every line,
The stories etched will always shine.
In mirrors' depths, we meet our past,
Forgotten faces, ever cast.

Lost and Found in a Drawer

In the depths of forgotten space,
Treasures hide in a secret place.
Old letters wrapped in yellowed bands,
Stories written by trembling hands.

A photograph with edges worn,
Memories of love, and some lost and torn.
A trinket here, a coin from the past,
Echoes linger, shadows are cast.

Keychains from places I've never been,
In the quiet, the dust settles thin.
A half-spun tale of life's fleeting hues,
Glimpses of moments I long to choose.

Each item whispers, time's gentle thief,
In the drawer of dreams, I find my grief.
Yet hidden within, a spark of delight,
In memories cherished, the heart takes flight.

The Luggage I Never Carried

In the corner, it waits, untouched,
A suitcase closed, dreams still clutched.
Tags still hang, destinations bold,
Stories untold, waiting to unfold.

The weight of the world locked inside,
Places I dreamt of, but never did ride.
Cities alive with laughter and tears,
A journey deferred through all of the years.

Dust collects on the fabric's skin,
Wanderlust wanes as silence creeps in.
Handles worn but never held tight,
An empty vessel, lost in the night.

Imagined horizons, forgotten by time,
The call of adventure, a silent chime.
What ifs and maybes packed into seams,
Every corner waiting for traveler dreams.

Whispering Walls of Old Rooms

With peeling paint and stories old,
Whispers linger, secrets told.
Every creak of the aging floor,
Echoes of laughter, lost evermore.

The sunlight dances through dusty panes,
Casting shadowy memories that remain.
Each corner holds a tale in bloom,
Life once breathed within this room.

Faded wallpaper with patterns worn,
Framed moments of joy, longing, and scorn.
Soft sighs of the past in the gentle air,
In these spaces, love lingers rare.

Walls that harbor both heartache and bliss,
Captured within the silence, a kiss.
They stand as sentinels, proud and tall,
Guardian of stories hidden in the hall.

Yesterday's Garden Overgrown

Once vibrant blooms filled every space,
Now wild weeds in a tangled embrace.
Nature's whispers have turned to shouts,
In the garden, where hope once sprouted.

Faded petals lie scattered near,
Memories of laughter now choked by fear.
An iron gate rusty, swinging slow,
Where sunlight once danced, shadows now grow.

Tree branches reach for the sun's warm kiss,
While thorns bite back where beauty once is.
A forgotten path winds through the thicket,
Each step taken, a heart-bound ticket.

Yet in the chaos, a hint of grace,
Wildflowers bloom in their untamed place.
A reminder that life will always renew,
Even in gardens of yesterday's hues.

When the Sun Sets on Us

When the sun sets on the horizon's line,
Shadows stretch, and hearts intertwine.
Whispers of dusk, sweet and low,
Promise of dreams in the twilight's glow.

Golden rays dance, bidding goodbye,
Painting the sky with a soft, warm sigh.
In that moment, we breathe as one,
Under the blanket of night begun.

Stars awaken in the velvet sky,
Guardians of secrets, they hear our sigh.
Fingers entwined, we stand in awe,
As the world fades under night's gentle law.

Together we wander through shadows deep,
Finding solace in the vows we keep.
When the night calls, we answer true,
For love's light shines in the darkest blue.

And as the sun sets on memories made,
In every heartbeat, our love won't fade.
Forever in twilight, hand in hand,
We embrace the night, a promised land.

Unpacked Suitcases of the Soul

Inside the mind, we carry our weight,
Unpacked suitcases, emotions and fate.
Dreams left behind, echoes of flight,
Silent reminders in the dark of night.

Worn out tags tell stories untold,
Of laughter and tears and moments bold.
What do we leave when we journey afar?
Pieces of us, like a shooting star.

Dust settles where the heart does roam,
Memories linger, they whisper of home.
Identities shift as we seek to find,
Unraveling threads of the heart and mind.

Cultures collide, and we dance with grace,
In every encounter, we leave a trace.
With every suitcase, a lesson we learn,
The soul of a traveler, forever we yearn.

So here's to the journeys we take every day,
In unpacked suitcases, we find our way.
Each moment a treasure, each memory gold,
In the map of our lives, our stories unfold.

Ghosts of Unspoken Words

In the silence, shadows softly creep,
Ghosts of words we wish to keep.
Whispers linger in the midnight air,
Remnants of truths left bare.

Thoughts unshared echo in our minds,
Heavy with longing, love that binds.
Every glance holds a tale untold,
A treasure of feelings, yearning bold.

Fears hold us, keep our voices still,
Yet deep inside, the heart has will.
Will we break free of this haunting chain?
To speak of love, to let go of pain?

A moment of courage, a chance to say,
Words of the heart, come what may.
For in the light, the shadows will fade,
Releasing the ghosts that silence had made.

So let the echoes rise to the skies,
For in spoken truths, freedom lies.
With every heartbeat, let silence cease,
Embrace the power, find your peace.

Tides of Time Adrift

The tides of time swirl and flow,
Carrying moments, high and low.
Each wave a memory, drifting afar,
Guided by the light of a distant star.

Seasons change with the moon's soft gaze,
Days slip by in a hazy daze.
Caught in the currents, we ride the stream,
Chasing the whispers of a forgotten dream.

Footprints fade on the sandy shore,
Lost in time, like days before.
Each heartbeat echoes in the sea's embrace,
A dance with the ages, a timeless chase.

Yet in the ebb, there's hope anew,
The promise of dawn, the morning dew.
For every ending births a start,
The tides of time bind us in the heart.

So let us sail on this ocean wide,
With love as our compass, and dreams as our guide.
Through calm and storm, we shall drift,
Forever united, a timeless gift.

Dreams That Slipped Through Fingers

In the quiet night, they fade away,
Whispers of hope, lost in dismay.
Chasing shadows, we reach and cling,
Yet like water, they slip, they sting.

Fleeting moments slip through our grasp,
Flickering dreams in destiny's clasp.
We reach for stars above so bright,
But they dim as we lose our sight.

Once vivid colors, now shades of gray,
Echoes of wishes that couldn't stay.
Laughter and joy, like smoke in the air,
Elusive visions, too precious to bear.

A heart once full, now an empty sigh,
We mourn the dreams that dared to fly.
Through memories, we wander and roam,
Yearning for dreams that felt like home.

Yet in the darkness, a glimmer remains,
A spark of hope amid all the chains.
With every dawn comes a chance to mend,
To catch new dreams, and let them ascend.

Pages Torn from Life's Book

In the wind, pages scatter and dance,
Stories of laughter, love, and chance.
Torn from the spine, drifting away,
Fragments of life, lost in dismay.

Ink stains, a trace of who we were,
Memories linger, lost in a blur.
Turning the leaves reveals hidden scars,
Silent echoes of battles and wars.

Each chapter written, a tale untold,
Of dreams once cherished, now feeling cold.
Life's narrative woven with joy and pain,
In the heart, the remnants still remain.

As dusk descends, shadows take flight,
The book of our lives, a fading light.
Yet in the margins, hope leaves its mark,
A promise of dawn, a spark in the dark.

So gather the pages, piecing anew,
For life is a journey, ever askew.
In every tear, a lesson unfurls,
A testament to our vibrant worlds.

Silent Farewells at Dusk

At twilight's door, we bid adieu,
Words unspoken, yet feelings true.
A glance, a smile, says what we feel,
In silence, our hearts begin to heal.

The setting sun casts shadows long,
An echo of love, a bittersweet song.
Memories linger, wrapped in the dusk,
Tender moments held close, a hidden musk.

With each soft sigh, the night draws near,
Whispers of parting, a trace of fear.
But in the stillness, there's beauty found,
In silent farewells, a love profound.

Stars appear, a gentle embrace,
Illuminating dreams we dare to chase.
Though paths may diverge, we're not alone,
In shadows of dusk, our hearts have grown.

So let us hold the night close and dear,
For each goodbye brings a new frontier.
In the quiet, warmth through sorrow flows,
Silent farewells bloom like a rose.

In the Company of Silence

Amidst the noise, a stillness calls,
In whispers soft, the silence falls.
Draped in shadows, the echoes fade,
A tranquil peace, the world displayed.

Thoughts unravel in the quiet space,
Finding solace in a gentle embrace.
Between the words, the heart can speak,
In silence found, we're never weak.

Moments linger, profound and deep,
In the arms of silence, secrets keep.
Beneath the surface, emotions flow,
In the company of silence, we grow.

When chaos reigns, the calm persists,
In reflection's light, we find our tryst.
Connections forged in serene delight,
In stillness, we bask, in endless night.

So cherish the silence, let it thrive,
For in its presence, we feel alive.
In the company of stillness, we're free,
A sacred bond, just you and me.

Paintings of What Could Have Been

In quiet corners dreams reside,
Fingers trace on canvas wide.
Colors blend, emotions pour,
Scenes of life that were before.

Whispers of a distant time,
Painted words in silent rhyme.
Moments caught between the hues,
Shadows whispering of lost views.

Each brushstroke tells a tale anew,
A life imagined, bright and true.
Yet fading softly with the light,
A canvas dimmed, out of sight.

Hope and sorrow intertwined,
In every piece, a soul confined.
Yet beauty lingers in the pain,
Artistry from joy and strain.

What could have been, forever stays,
In paintings where our heartstrings play.
A gallery of dreams unfolds,
In vibrant shades, our story told.

The Stars We Never Counted

In the velvet night we lay,
Counting stars that drift away.
Each twinkle holds a silent wish,
Moments lost in fate's full swish.

Eyes cast skyward, hearts aglow,
Dreams entangled in the flow.
But galaxies afar remain,
Whispers caught in time's harsh rain.

We reached for worlds we could not touch,
Infinite cosmos, oh so much.
Yet in the dark, our spirits soared,
In the night sky, we explored.

Constellations danced with fate,
Guiding us through love and hate.
The stars we dreamed are still unseen,
In darkness bright, our hopes convene.

And though we drift from sight to sight,
Our souls ignite the endless night.
Every star, a story spun,
In the cosmos, we're all one.

Worn Paths Leading Away

Footsteps echo on the ground,
Worn paths where hearts once were found.
Whispers linger in the air,
Memories of love laid bare.

Twists and turns tell tales untold,
Of journeys taken, brave and bold.
Each stone and leaf bears witness true,
To dreams that once in sunlight grew.

But shadows creep where light once shone,
Paths leading to the great unknown.
We tread alone, yet still we yearn,
For warmth of hearts we can't return.

Yet traces of the past remain,
In each step, both joy and pain.
Worn paths beckon, soft and sweet,
A journey shared with love discreet.

As we walk our separate ways,
In twilight's glow, the memory stays.
On worn paths, we find a guide,
To carry us with love and pride.

The Ghosts of Forgotten Laughter

In halls where echoes softly creep,
Ghosts of laughter, memories deep.
Fading sunlight paints the walls,
Once lively, now a silence calls.

Footsteps dance in twilight's glow,
Fleeting whispers from long ago.
In every corner, shadows play,
Where joy was bright, now shades of gray.

Laughter lingers in the dust,
In every heart, a bond of trust.
Yet time erodes those joyous sounds,
Leaving traces where love abounds.

We tiptoe through the echoes clear,
Seeking solace in the near.
Though ghosts of joy may haunt our days,
In their whispers, love still stays.

So let the past remind our hearts,
Of laughter's gift and all its parts.
For in the silence, we reclaim,
The echoes of forgotten names.

The Silence of Abandonment

In the corners, shadows creep,
Lonely echoes, secrets deep.
Whispers lost, the air turned cold,
A story faded, never told.

Windows shut, no light breaks through,
Memories haunt, not one is new.
A heart that beats, yet feels no sound,
In silence, sorrow's tightly wound.

Ghosts of laughter drift away,
As time's cruel hands begin to sway.
A playground once, now silent ground,
In every creak, a pain profound.

Once a home, where joy would dance,
Now shadows steal each fleeting chance.
The whispers fade with each new night,
In the silence, loss takes flight.

But hope still flickers, dim and small,
In the silence, it may call.
For even in the darkest place,
Resilience fights, finds its grace.

Unfinished Letters in the Drawer

Dusty papers, words unsent,
Hidden feelings, time ill-spent.
Ink that dried before it flew,
Thoughts of love I never knew.

Promises penned in trembling hands,
Fragments of dreams, slipped like sands.
Each letter holds a breath of pain,
Stories waiting, longing to explain.

Faded ink and crumpled lines,
Hope laid bare in tangled signs.
A heart that wanted to be heard,
Now silent, trapped within a word.

Sealed in time, a soul's desire,
Caught in memory's gentle fire.
If only courage found a way,
To break the silence, stop the sway.

But here they lie, untouched, forlorn,
The echoes of a love, now worn.
In every crease, a missed embrace,
Unfinished letters, lost in space.

Faded Footprints in the Sand

Upon the beach, where tides align,
Footprints linger, a silent sign.
Each a story, time has passed,
Yet whispers of the moments last.

Waves lap gently, soft and low,
Washing memories, ebb and flow.
A dance of dreams beneath the sun,
Fading fast, but never done.

Shells tell tales of journeys wide,
Of hearts once bound, now cast aside.
In every grain, a love once shared,
A fleeting glance, a soul laid bare.

The sunset bleeds in hues of red,
Where silence reigns, and all is said.
Yet still, the footprints whisper on,
In their fading, life goes on.

Tomorrow's tide will hide away,
The traces left from yesterday.
But in the heart, they'll ever stand,
Faded footprints in the sand.

The Unraveled Thread

In every stitch, a tale is spun,
Life's fabric fades, comes undone.
Colors blur, and patterns fray,
As dreams dissolve and slip away.

Once a tapestry of bright designs,
Now unravels in tangled lines.
Hopes once woven, now fallen flat,
The art of living, where's it at?

Fingers grasp at frayed remains,
Holding tight to bittersweet chains.
But with each tug, a thread does part,
Revealing scars upon the heart.

Yet there is beauty in disorder,
A chance to weave a new border.
With every knot, new paths are made,
In chaos, stories unafraid.

So gather threads, and start anew,
From every tear, create what's true.
For in the weave of life's own hand,
The unravels forge a sturdier strand.

The Last Page Left Unturned

In twilight's glow the stories fade,
A book of dreams, a life replayed.
The ink is dry, the words sit still,
What lies ahead, a void to fill.

Beneath the moon, my thoughts drift wide,
Each chapter close, I must abide.
Yet memories linger, soft and sweet,
A whispered promise, a heart's heartbeat.

I trace the lines, I seek the end,
A tale unfinished, a broken bend.
With every pause the silence grows,
What do I seek? The story knows.

One final breath to take me far,
Where endings meet the distant star.
So here I sit, my thoughts unwind,
The last page waits, the truth I find.

In every sigh, a love once real,
The last page holds what I conceal.
A journey's end, but not in vain,
For every loss, a sweet refrain.

Pieces of a Shattered Past

Fragments fall like autumn leaves,
Memories clung to like old thieves.
Each broken shard reflects a face,
A whispered name in empty space.

Once vibrant colors fade to gray,
A canvas torn, now led astray.
Yet in the cracks, a glimpse of light,
Resilience blooms in endless night.

Through corridors of yesterday,
I gather pieces, lost along the way.
With every step, I stitch and mend,
To make a whole from what won't blend.

Time walks slowly, yet it is fleet,
A bittersweet, relentless beat.
I hold the past in gentle hands,
As echoes dance upon the sands.

The puzzle waits, a story yet,
In every scar, my heart beset.
In shattered past, I find the grace,
To build anew, to find my place.

Where Shadows Gather

In corners dim where silence sleeps,
The shadows gather, secrets keep.
They stretch and weave, a dance so sly,
In half-lit rooms where whispers lie.

The air grows thick, the night draws near,
With every sound, the pulse of fear.
Yet in the gloom, a spark remains,
A flicker of hope that ever gains.

Beneath the weight of silent screams,
The heart still dares to dream new dreams.
A flickering light, a guiding star,
In darkest times, it's never far.

Among the shades, there's life anew,
With every dawn, the shadows rue.
For in the light, we find our way,
And mend the night, reclaim the day.

So when the twilight starts to creep,
And shadows form, our souls to sweep,
I'll stand my ground, let courage rise,
For where they gather, hope defies.

Lingering Whispers in the Hall

In faded rooms where echoes dwell,
The whispers weave a gentle spell.
With every creak the stories sigh,
In shadows cast, the past flies by.

Upon the walls, old laughter lingers,
The ghostly touch of soft, warm fingers.
Each corner holds a tale untold,
Of love and loss, a heart of gold.

Beneath the hush, a heartbeat's thrum,
A symphony of what's to come.
In every breath, the echoes call,
The sweetest sound in quiet hall.

The past and present intertwine,
In each soft whisper, truth aligns.
Each memory keeps the flame alive,
In lingering tales, we thrive, we strive.

So in the hall, I'll pause to hear,
The whispers draw me ever near.
For in their song, I find my way,
The heart remembers, come what may.

The Half-Remembered Road

Along the winding path I tread,
Whispers of the past are spread.
Faded signs and shadows loom,
Echoes call from distant gloom.

Each step unveils a hidden tale,
Ghostly tales that never pale.
Footprints left by those long gone,
In the twilight, I press on.

Memories dance like autumn leaves,
Carried softly on the breeze.
Fragments lost yet still so near,
Relics of a yesteryear.

The road bends under silver light,
Stars ignite the velvet night.
With every choice, the journey flows,
To places only heart knows.

And so I wander, heart in hand,
Tracing routes where love once spanned.
The half-remembered, ever sweet,
In dreams where past and present meet.

A Canvas of Departed Moments

Brush strokes paint a fleeting scene,
Colors vibrant, edges mean.
Captured glances, laughter shared,
Memories linger, hearts laid bare.

Each hue tells of stories lost,
Of moments cherished at great cost.
In every corner, shadows play,
Fleeting whispers of yesterday.

Time has donned its canvas gray,
Yet beauty blooms within decay.
Fingers trace the lines of fate,
Where joy and sorrow intertwine, innate.

The artist's heart remains confined,
To fragments of a life entwined.
A canvas rich with colors bright,
Reflects both darkness and the light.

So linger here among the shades,
In every brush, a memory fades.
A canvas where the past unfolds,
Imprints of the brave and bold.

Ashes of Unremembered Dreams

In quiet corners of the night,
Ashes smolder, dimly bright.
Dreams once danced like fireflies,
Now rest beneath forgotten skies.

Whispers echo in the dark,
Pale reflections, a fading spark.
What was once a vibrant flight,
Now shrouded in a veil of night.

Each ember tells a tale untold,
Fragments of a wish gone cold.
Fleeting moments, time's cruel hand,
Turns bright hopes into shifting sand.

Yet in these ashes, life will bloom,
From the remnants, scents of gloom.
New dreams kindle, sparks ignite,
Transforming shadows into light.

So gather close the scattered dust,
In future's embrace, we trust.
Ashes fade, yet flames survive,
In every end, new dreams arrive.

Timeworn Treasures of the Heart

Nestled deep within the chest,
Lie treasures time has repressed.
Jewels of laughter, tears like rain,
Each a story, joy, and pain.

A worn-out photo, edges frayed,
Captures moments we once made.
Time has etched its gentle mark,
Yet love remains a vibrant spark.

The letters yellowed, ink half-faded,
Words of passion never jaded.
Promises whispered in twilight's glow,
Timeworn treasures continue to flow.

Through storms of life, they stand so true,
Strengthened by the trials we knew.
Memory's embrace will never part,
Casting shadows on the heart.

And as the years steadily move,
These treasures hold a timeless groove.
Within them lies a life well-spun,
All the battles lost and won.

The Weight of Forgotten Things

In shadows where memories lie,
Whispers of dreams that once soared high.
Time has scattered them like dust,
Left behind, their fading trust.

Through corridors of muted sighs,
Echoes of laughter, distant cries.
Each trinket holds a silent tale,
Of moments cherished, now grown pale.

Beneath layers of unkempt years,
Lies a weight of bottled tears.
Silent burdens that we carry,
Reminders of the times we tarry.

In the corners where darkness creeps,
A tapestry of what time keeps.
Forgotten things, yet not erased,
Their essence in our hearts still placed.

To lift the weight, we must recall,
Embrace the joy, despite the fall.
For in the shards of what once was,
Lies the truth of loving because.

Silhouettes of a Closed Door

Eclipsed by night, a door stands still,
Casting shadows, a ghostly thrill.
What lies beyond, we cannot see,
Fragments of what used to be.

Breezes whisper through the crack,
Lost tales linger but won't come back.
Silhouettes dance in the dim light,
Fleeting glimpses of forgotten night.

Faded memories cling to the frame,
Each marking a piece of the same.
Hands once reached to turn the knob,
Now hold the echoes of a sob.

A space once full, now quiet bare,
Every breath stirs the stagnant air.
What if the world beyond it waits,
To weave anew our tangled fates?

A decision rests in the heart,
To leave behind or make a start.
A closed door haunts, but does inspire,
For hope ignites a dormant fire.

Fragments of an Old Heart

Scattered pieces beneath the bed,
Whispers of love long since shed.
Each fragment tells a story bold,
Of laughter shared and dreams foretold.

Cracked edges, sharp yet tender too,
Memories lost, yet feeling new.
Time has weathered this old frame,
Yet passion's spark still fuels the flame.

Among the shards, the light still gleams,
Faded echoes of forgotten dreams.
Bestowed with grace from days gone by,
A heart that learned to weep and fly.

In every splinter, a lesson lies,
To love again, to rise, to try.
Though battered, weary, worn by fate,
A heart still beats, it's never late.

With open hands, we gather close,
The fragments sing, they love the most.
For in their dance, we find the art,
Of mending wounds within the heart.

Through the Dusty Window

A veil of dust on glass so thin,
Shows the world where dreams begin.
Outside, the colors blush and play,
Yet here, we watch them drift away.

Raindrops race on windowpanes,
Whispers of soft, forgotten rains.
A scene of life, both wild and free,
Yet trapped within this room, we see.

Each breath is heavy with the past,
Moments that slipped away too fast.
Silhouettes of what could have been,
Glimmers that fade, we shudder, spin.

To peer beyond, we must release,
The weight of grief to find our peace.
Through dusty panes, we search for light,
To break the chains of endless night.

Outside, the world awaits us still,
With open arms and hopeful thrill.
So let us wipe the glass and trust,
To step beyond the veil of dust.

Portraits Left Unframed

In shadows you stand, so still,
Your eyes whisper tales untold,
Each crease a memory, a thrill,
A canvas of moments, both young and old.

Brushstrokes linger in the air,
Colors blend where silence sings,
Forgotten dreams of love and care,
Hang loosely from forgotten strings.

Your laughter dances in the light,
As echoes of joy begin to fade,
A portrait caught in twilight's bite,
In time's embrace, we are remade.

Yet still, the frame remains unbound,
With stories trapped in fading hue,
And in this space, lost dreams are found,
In every shade, of me and you.

So here we stand, with hearts unchained,
Within the art that we confess,
Our lives a canvas, uncontained,
Portraits left unframed, we bless.

The Art of Letting Go

In whispered winds, the past departs,
Like kites released into the sky,
We learn to mend our weary hearts,
As memories wave their last goodbye.

The burdens lift with gentle grace,
Each weight a lesson learned, undone,
We find our peace in empty space,
Where once the storm raged, now there's sun.

Each moment's thread begins to fray,
But in the threadbare, hope resides,
To weave anew, we find our way,
In every tear, the courage hides.

The canvas spreads before our eyes,
A palette rich with vibrant hues,
In letting go, our spirits rise,
To dance among the morning dew.

In every sigh, the chains release,
We learn the art of letting go,
A tranquil heart finds sweet embrace,
As life unfolds in endless flow.

A Diary of Silent Goodbyes

Upon these pages, shadows dwell,
In written words, emotions flow,
Each ink-stained line a gentle farewell,
A diary of silent goodbyes to stow.

The weight of years in tender turns,
Each chapter kissed by fleeting time,
A flicker of ache, as memory yearns,
To hold what once was, like a rhyme.

Between the margins, love's embrace,
The echoes of laughter, bittersweet,
A journey traced in time and space,
Where paths diverge, yet hearts still meet.

With every closure, hope ignites,
A spark of light in the darkened night,
The diary reveals our hidden fights,
And yet, in the silence, we find our flight.

In whispered thoughts, the pages turn,
Each goodbye a seed, a chance to grow,
So in this ink, our stories burn,
A diary of silent goodbyes we know.

Leaves of the Old Maple

Among the branches, secrets sway,
The old maple stands, wise and tall,
Leaves whisper tales of night and day,
Their dance a tribute, an earthy call.

In spring's embrace, new life begins,
Emerald dreams unfurl and stretch,
But autumn's breath, it softly spins,
A tapestry of gold, a gentle etch.

With every fall, a lesson learned,
In letting go, we find our song,
For each leaf dropped, a heart is turned,
As seasons shift, we all belong.

The roots run deep, and branches wide,
In every circle, life renews,
The old maple holds the love inside,
And stands through storms, when the sky is bruised.

So gather 'round and hear the lore,
Of leaves that dance and whispers flow,
In every rustle, we find much more,
The stories held in the old maple.

Tattered Maps of Memory Lane

Faded edges, worn and frayed,
A journey through the past conveyed.
Each fold reveals a story true,
Of laughter shared, and skies so blue.

Footprints linger on the ground,
In whispered winds, their echoes sound.
With every step, the heart remembers,
The warmth of love in smoky embers.

Crimson leaves in autumn's dance,
Breathe life into a fleeting glance.
Old songs carried through the air,
Remind us all how much we care.

Yet shadows weave through sunlit paths,
A bittersweet of what still lasts.
In tattered maps, we find our way,
Through time's embrace, we choose to stay.

So hold these maps, though worn and torn,
In every line, a tale reborn.
For memory's road often bends,
And leads us home, where love transcends.

Portraits of Departed Dreams

In frames of gold, dreams once framed,
In silent halls, they feel unnamed.
With every brushstroke, memories sigh,
Of hopes that linger, and dreams that fly.

Echoes of laughter paint the air,
Yet time has rendered them quite rare.
Faded hues of what could be,
Now haunt the corners silently.

Whispers of wishes in twilight's glow,
A gallery of might-have-been, we know.
Each portrait tells a story lost,
Of roads not taken, of love's great cost.

Through clouds of doubt, the visions dance,
We wander still, in hopes of chance.
But shadows play in dimmed light's gleam,
A reflection of our faded dream.

Yet in this space, they still reside,
Our cherished hopes, forever bide.
For even when dreams fade to mist,
In our hearts, they still exist.

When the Clock Strikes Silence

In the stillness, time takes pause,
A gentle breath without a cause.
When seconds stop and echoes cease,
The world suspends in quiet peace.

Shadows stretch across the floor,
As moments linger, wanting more.
Whispers fade in candlelight,
When the clock strikes, we greet the night.

Drifting thoughts, like feathers, fall,
In this tranquil, hallowed hall.
Dreams awaken, softly spoken,
In the silence, hearts unbroken.

Time itself seems to relent,
In fleeting breaths, joy is lent.
For when the clock can hush its sound,
A deeper truth is often found.

So in those hours, let us dwell,
Where silence holds its gentle spell.
For in still moments, we can see,
The beauty in our reverie.

Between Here and There

A space exists, unseen yet near,
Where dreams are born and disappear.
Between the lines of now and then,
We craft our paths, we rise again.

In twilight's glow, the heart can roam,
To places that feel like a home.
With every heartbeat, worlds collide,
In this in-between, we confide.

A step towards the unknown waits,
In courage found, we open gates.
The map unfolds, with every breath,
A dance with life, not bound by death.

Through whispers of the breeze we hear,
The stories of all who ventured here.
Between hope and despair's claim,
We find our fire, we fan the flame.

So let us dwell in this sweet space,
Where dreams and doubts find their grace.
For in this moment, vast and rare,
We live our truth, between here and there.

Pieces of a Distant Journey

In the shadows of the night,
Footsteps echo soft and light.
Memories drift like whispered dreams,
Across the starlit silver streams.

Paths once taken, stories told,
Winds of change, both fierce and bold.
Fragments of time, scattered wide,
Guide the heart where secrets hide.

With every step, the past entwined,
In the fabric of the mind.
Threads of hope and threads of pain,
Stitched together, they remain.

Through valleys deep and mountains high,
Finding truths as the years go by.
Each piece a token, each voice a guide,
Upon this journey, side by side.

In every corner, a lesson learned,
From every flame, our spirit burned.
We gather pieces, hold them tight,
For in our hearts, they shine so bright.

A Melody of Things Unspoken

In the silence, a soft refrain,
Notes of longing, sweetly plain.
Words unsaid float in the air,
Echoes of a hidden care.

With every glance, a story hides,
In the shadows, where love abides.
Feelings dance, a gentle tune,
In the night beneath the moon.

Fingers brush like whispered sighs,
Crafting dreams that never die.
In every pause, a world unknown,
A melody that feels like home.

When hearts collide, the music swells,
In quiet places, magic dwells.
Unraveled threads, connect and weave,
A tapestry that we believe.

Though words may fail, the heart will sing,
In the spaces, love takes wing.
Let the silence be our guide,
In this dance, where hopes abide.

The Parting Gift of Remembrance

As daylight fades, memories spark,
In tender moments, a silent arc.
Laughter echoes, shadows play,
A parting gift at the end of day.

Seasons change, yet hearts remain,
Carried softly, like gentle rain.
Each goodbye, a door ajar,
Where love lingers, a guiding star.

Fragments of time glide through the years,
In every joy and in each tear.
A treasure chest, emotions stored,
In silence held, and never ignored.

We weave the stories, bright and bold,
A legacy that can't grow old.
In every heartbeat, you live on,
The parting gift, forever strong.

As twilight falls, I hold you near,
In whispered thoughts, you reappear.
Through every memory, love persists,
A gentle touch, a fleeting kiss.

Chasing Phantoms of Life's Choices

In fleeting moments, shadows play,
Chasing phantoms, they slip away.
Paths diverge in misty light,
Echoes linger, out of sight.

Every choice, a dance with fate,
In the mirror, we contemplate.
What might have been haunts the soul,
A restless heart, searching for whole.

Through winding roads, we seek the best,
In the journey, we find the rest.
Each decision, a step to take,
In the tapestry, life's sweet mistake.

Phantoms whisper, urging delay,
Yet the present, it calls to stay.
In the dance of time, we sway,
Caught between the past and day.

With open hearts, we find our way,
Through the shadows, come what may.
For every choice a lesson learned,
In chasing phantoms, our spirits burned.

Echoes of Yesterday

In the silence, whispers call,
Memories dance, rise and fall.
Fading images in the light,
Echoes of dreams, lost to night.

Pictures linger, time's embrace,
Yearning hearts in empty space.
Once cherished souls, now mere shades,
Echoes of love fade, slowly fade.

In every corner, shadows play,
Stirring thoughts of yesterday.
A gentle sigh, a fleeting glance,
In dreams, we find a second chance.

Footsteps linger on the stairs,
Carrying tales, unspoken cares.
The past a quilt, frayed and worn,
In echoes bright, new hopes are born.

Yet in the glow of evening's hue,
The past will weave our story true.
In the silence, we shall find,
Echoes of yesterday entwined.

Shadows in the Attic

In the attic, dust collects,
Whispers of what time forgets.
Old trunks hold stories, tightly bound,
Shadows dance with barely a sound.

Tattered letters, words once spoken,
Secrets linger, hearts unbroken.
Photographs in faded frames,
Relive the joy, the tears, the names.

The beams hold echoes of laughter's glee,
Faint traces of who we used to be.
In the darkness, memories swirl,
Shadows of each forgotten whirl.

Dust motes twinkle in sunlight's grace,
Reflecting time we can't replace.
Each sigh of wood has tales to unveil,
Shadows whisper, a haunting trail.

As twilight falls, we hold on tight,
To shadows that dance in the fading light.
In the attic, we find our truth,
Whispers of innocence, echoes of youth.

Fragments of a Forgotten Past

Fragments scattered on the floor,
Echoes from a time before.
Shattered dreams and fleeting days,
In whispered winds, their spirit stays.

Each broken piece tells a tale,
Of laughter lost, of love's frail.
Time's embrace, gentle yet cruel,
Fragments shimmer in history's pool.

Dust-covered trinkets, stories hold,
Whispers of courage, brave and bold.
In shadows cast, the past will gleam,
Fragments unite in a silent dream.

Secrets woven in the thread,
Events that glow though often tread.
Each piece a part of who we are,
Fragments of past, our guiding star.

As seasons change and years unwind,
Fragments linger, love entwined.
In the tapestry of life, we sing,
Fragments unite in the joy they bring.

The Weight of Unsaid Goodbyes

Words linger in the heavy air,
Unsaid goodbyes, a silent stare.
Promises fade like morning mist,
In aching hearts, they still persist.

Each moment shared, a fleeting spark,
Now wrapped in shadows, cold and dark.
Lingering thoughts of what could be,
The weight of love, too vast to see.

In heavy hearts, regrets reside,
Unsaid goodbyes we try to hide.
Echoing softly, a haunting tune,
In memories, we find our ruin.

Time flows on, but still we wait,
For words unsaid to meet their fate.
In the silence, they begin to rise,
The weight of love, of unsaid goodbyes.

Yet in our hearts, they find their place,
A bittersweet dance, a soft embrace.
With every tear, we learn to fly,
Transcending the weight of goodbyes.

Footprints on a Winding Path

Each step we take is marked with grace,
On winding trails we find our place.
The whispers of the trees above,
Guard secrets of our hidden love.

A journey shaped by twists and bends,
Where every turn becomes a friend.
The shadows dance, the sunlight plays,
In every challenge, hope still stays.

Through valleys deep and mountains high,
We chase the moments as they fly.
With every footprint, stories grow,
On paths untraveled, hearts will know.

Together we face the morning mist,
In every dawn, there's an enchanting twist.
With open hearts, we take the leap,
Embracing memories we will keep.

And when we reach the journey's end,
We'll cherish every curve, my friend.
Our footprints scattered, far and wide,
In nature's arms, we will abide.

Lost Letters in the Drawer

In the quiet of the night, I find,
Old letters waiting, intertwined.
Each word a brush of faded ink,
A glimpse of thoughts that make me think.

Forgotten whispers from days of yore,
They beckon softly, like a lore.
Wrapped in memories, love and pain,
A treasure trove chased by the rain.

Each page unfolds a distant dream,
Of hopes and wishes, like a stream.
In papered folds, emotions swirl,
A silent dance, a lover's whirl.

I read the lines, my heart takes flight,
As words illuminate the night.
These lost letters, fragile yet bold,
Unlock the stories they once told.

A tapestry of life displayed,
In faded ink, we were betrayed.
Yet in the drawer, they remain,
A testament to love's sweet pain.

The Silence After the Storm

When thunder fades and winds subside,
A quiet hush, the world's confide.
The earth, now washed, breathes a new air,
In stillness found, there's peace to share.

Raindrops linger on blades of grass,
A fleeting moment, it will pass.
The sky, a canvas of soft gray,
Embraces hope for a bright new day.

In the silence, memories churn,
Lessons learned, as embers burn.
Each heartbeat echoes in the calm,
A soothing balm, a healing psalm.

Nature whispers tales untold,
In shadows cast, its wisdom bold.
The light returns, a soft embrace,
Reminding us of every grace.

After the storm, we stand and see,
The beauty found in tragedy.
In silence, we begin anew,
A world reborn, resilient and true.

Those Frayed Edges of Time

In the fabric of our lives, we find,
The frayed edges that define our mind.
Each thread a story, worn and torn,
A testament to love, hope reborn.

Moments lost in the weave of days,
Fading colors, forgotten ways.
Yet in each tear, a lesson grows,
A deeper truth that life bestows.

We gather pieces, patching our hearts,
In the quilt of time, we play our parts.
With every stitch, new memories bloom,
Amidst the chaos, we find our room.

The edges fray, but do not break,
They whisper wisdom in every ache.
A vintage tale woven so fine,
In the embrace of those frayed lines.

Through trials faced, we'll stand our ground,
In the tapestry of life, we're bound.
Each fraying edge, a mark of grace,
A journey shared in this sacred space.

The Scent of Longing

In cool twilight, whispers call,
Fragrant dreams begin to fall.
Echoes of a soft embrace,
Memories that time can't trace.

Petals drift with gentle grace,
Every scent a hidden space.
Yearning hearts, a sweet refrain,
Searching where the lost remain.

A breeze carries soft desire,
Hearts ignite like fleeting fire.
In the shadows, hopes ignite,
Guided by the stars at night.

With every waft, we recall,
Moments lost, yet still stand tall.
Through the pain, we learn to cope,
In the fragrance, lies our hope.

The scent of longing fills the air,
Fleeting thoughts beyond compare.
A journey paved with softest sighs,
Where love lingers and never dies.

A Change in the Breeze

A sudden shift, the world awakes,
Nature stirs and softly shakes.
Whispers tangled in the trees,
A promise carried in the breeze.

New horizons greet the dawn,
Old regrets, now gently gone.
Gentle winds bring forth the change,
Time to grow, to feel, to range.

Embrace the shift, let shadows fade,
In the light, new dreams are made.
Butterflies in graceful flight,
Hope reborn with morning light.

Waves of air, a beckoning call,
To rise up, to stand up tall.
Every gust, a chance anew,
In the breeze, our spirits grew.

Seasons shift, but hearts remain,
In the dance of joy and pain.
With each breath, we greet the day,
A change in the breeze paves the way.

The Echoes We Don't Speak Of

In silence linger words unsaid,
Haunting thoughts, a thread of dread.
Embers glow in hidden space,
Memories we can't erase.

Familiar laughter fades away,
In the shadows, echoes play.
Stolen glances, fleeting sighs,
Whispers lost in boundless skies.

Time has blurred our shared refrain,
Yet still, we feel the ghost of pain.
In every shadow, every heart,
Lingers hope we won't depart.

The past beckons, soft and low,
Yearning for the light to show.
Unspoken truths we try to hide,
Yet in silence, hearts collide.

So let us walk this path of gray,
Embrace the words we cannot say.
Through quiet nights, let spirits soar,
For echoes bind us evermore.

Memories Beneath the Surface

In ripples deep, the stories lie,
Hidden truths beneath the sky.
Fragments float on waters clear,
Each wave brings a dreamy tear.

Nostalgia dances on the shore,
Every glance reveals once more.
Echoes of a life once lived,
In the stillness, hearts forgive.

Beneath the calm, the past resides,
In depths where history hides.
Laughter haunts the sunlit waves,
In the silence, memory saves.

Time may fade, but can't erase,
The tender touch of love's embrace.
In each current, stories blend,
The surface hides, but never ends.

So dive deep, embrace the flow,
Find the tales it longs to show.
For memories beneath the surface,
Are treasures of a life with purpose.

Unseen Threads Tying Me Down

Invisible ties pull at my soul,
Whispers of doubt take their toll.
Every step feels heavy now,
Yet I search for a new way out.

Shadows of fear cling to my mind,
The path ahead is hard to find.
But through the struggle, I will rise,
And face the truth behind the lies.

Roots of regret dig deep in me,
Offering chains instead of free.
But hope glimmers like morning dew,
Reminding me to fight anew.

Beneath the weight, I sense a spark,
A flicker bright within the dark.
These unseen threads will break one day,
As I forge my own brave way.

And as I cut each binding line,
I rise again, stronger, divine.
With every scar, I'll stand my ground,
Embracing the freedom I have found.

Where the Echoes Fade

In the silence of a forgotten place,
Whispers linger, time's embrace.
Footsteps lost in the dusty air,
Memories vanish, fragile and rare.

Beneath the stars, the night wears thin,
Echoes of laughter, where to begin?
Faint melodies drift through the trees,
Stories woven in the gentle breeze.

The moonlight dances on crumbling stone,
Where shadows gather, I walk alone.
In the distance, faint calls retreat,
Leading me on with bittersweet.

Time erases what once was bright,
Yet I cherish every fleeting light.
In the quiet, I find my way,
With echoes fading, come what may.

And as the dawn brings a brand new day,
I'll carry the echoes, come what may.
In the stillness, I find my home,
Where the echoes fade, I will roam.

The Garden of Abandoned Hopes

In a garden where dreams no longer bloom,
Frayed petals whisper in darkening gloom.
Once vibrant colors now fade to gray,
Echoes of wishes lost along the way.

Beneath the thorns, an ache remains,
A tapestry woven with quiet pains.
Yet in the stillness, seeds lie in wait,
For sunlight's kiss to alter their fate.

Hope hangs heavy like mist in the air,
Nurtured by dreams too fragile to share.
With every breath, a promise is sown,
In the heart of the garden, love is grown.

Among the ruins of grief and despair,
I find a strength that blooms with care.
These abandoned hopes shall not be tossed,
For from the ashes, new dreams embossed.

So I'll tend to this garden of pain,
Water the roots and dance in the rain.
With each new start, I'll embrace the light,
In the garden of hopes, I shall take flight.

The Dust of Old Memories

In the attic, where memories lie,
Dust settles thick, forgotten by time.
Frayed photographs whisper of yore,
Moments once cherished now rest at the core.

Each memory floats on the air like a dream,
Fading away, yet bursting at the seam.
Voices echo from shadows long past,
Reminding me of joy that was never meant to last.

With every object, a story unfolds,
Of laughter and love, of secrets untold.
The dust of old memories clings to my skin,
A reminder of where I have been.

Yet every grain carries a weight of its own,
In the quietest corners, I am never alone.
For in the stillness, I find my peace,
In the dust of memories, my heart finds release.

So here I sit, wrapped in the past,
Finding beauty in stories that never last.
Each dusty relic, a treasure anew,
In the silence of memories, I find what is true.

Memory's Faded Stains

In the corners of my mind, they linger,
Whispers of laughter, shadows of old.
Time has dulled their vibrant color,
Yet their essence, still bold.

Pictures of faces, now blurred by years,
Echoes of joy, and moments of pain.
I trace the outlines, where love appears,
Holding on to what remains.

Each fleeting glance holds a story,
Framed in the silence that time bestows.
I cherish their fragments, and their glory,
Despite the inevitable close.

Grains of sand slip through the hourglass,
Fading softly, like words unsaid.
Yet in my heart, they gently pass,
Reviving dreams that once led.

These stains of memory, bittersweet,
Mark the canvas of my soul's retreat.
I gather the pieces, oh so dear,
And carry their whispers, year by year.

A Collection of Fragments

Scattered pieces of paper, torn,
Words woven in the fabric of time.
Each phrase a whisper, a thought reborn,
Echoing softly, like a silent rhyme.

Photographs tucked in a dusty chest,
Faces that smile, yet some feel strange.
I search for comfort, I seek for rest,
Among the mementos, amidst the change.

Old tickets and notes, a treasure trove,
Reminders of laughter, and dreams embraced.
In these small fragments, I gently rove,
Tracing the paths that time has graced.

A weathered map, routes long forgot,
Leads to places where sunsets kissed the sea.
In every fragment, lessons are taught,
A promise of who I used to be.

Curating these pieces, I find my voice,
In the chaos, a story to know.
Each fragment a step, a silent choice,
In the collection of moments that flow.

The Return of Old Ghosts

At twilight's caress, they drift back near,
Whispers of laughter, shadows that sway.
Haunting my dreams, they draw me near,
In echoes of night, they're here to stay.

Familiar faces, lost in the haze,
Remind me of paths once taken with grace.
In memories bright, I navigate the maze,
Through time's gentle hands, I recall each face.

Soft are their voices, a melancholic tune,
Dancing like leaves in the autumn air.
In the fading light of a silvered moon,
The old ghosts return, as if to care.

They linger in corners where silence sleeps,
In every shadow, a tale to weave.
These spectral friends, their promise keeps,
To remind me of what I should believe.

As dawn breaks soft, they start to fade,
Carrying whispers into the sun's embrace.
Yet in the stillness, I am not afraid,
For in my heart, they've left their trace.

Faded Photographs in Yellowed Books

In dusty corners, stories sleep,
Faded photographs in yellowed tomes.
Each page a memory, secrets to keep,
Whispers of lives, of hearths and homes.

Captured moments, now fragile and thin,
Time's gentle hand has worn them down.
But in each glance, I see where I've been,
In the silence, I wear a crown.

Faces once vibrant, now muted in hue,
Smiles that echo, laughter so sweet.
Through the ages, I journey anew,
Finding the past in the rhythm of feet.

The scent of paper, nostalgia and air,
In every chapter, a dream resides.
I wander through memories, unaware,
That time holds the truths that the heart confides.

These books tell stories, both bitter and bright,
Of love, loss, and moments that weave.
In faded photographs, I find my light,
And through their whispers, I still believe.

Songs of a Broken Promise

Whispers fade in empty halls,
Promises fall like autumn leaves.
Echoes linger, shadows call,
Fractured trust that never weaves.

In twilight's grasp, we stand still,
Ghosts of dreams drift through the air.
Heartbeats lost, against our will,
Words unspoken, masked in despair.

Once we danced, now we just wait,
Time rewinds, a cruel jest.
Memories heavy, burdened fate,
Yearning hearts that cannot rest.

A fractured song, a silent scream,
Hope unlocked, but doors are closed.
What was once a vibrant dream,
Now a tale of love proposed.

With every breath, the promise breaks,
A melody that fades away.
Yet still, within, a silence aches,
In shadows cast, we choose to stay.

Emptiness Wrapped in Leaves

Autumn whispers secrets low,
Leaves tumble, withered, and bare.
Nature seems to feel the blow,
As emptiness lingers in the air.

Branches stretch in cold dismay,
Lost in thoughts of summer's glow.
Each crisp breeze, a soft decay,
Echoes of a time we know.

Barefoot dreams now frozen tight,
Underneath a blanket white.
Hidden hopes in fading light,
All the world feels lost from sight.

Crimson colors, stark and bold,
Tell a tale of what has passed.
In every fold, a story told,
Of love, of loss, a silence cast.

Yet in stillness, beauty grows,
Underneath the weight of frost.
In the void, a longing glows,
For all that we have loved and lost.

Reflected in a Silent Tear

A single drop glints in the night,
Mirror to the heart's deep ache.
Whispers of love lost from sight,
In the stillness, sorrows wake.

Memories dance, shadows entwine,
Each tear tells a silent tale.
Hope flickers, then starts to shine,
In the darkest, windswept gale.

Every loss leaves a trace,
A photograph of what once was.
In the depths, we find our place,
In emptiness, a silent cause.

Time flows like a gentle stream,
Carrying whispers of the past.
In our hearts, the echoes dream,
Longing for the love we cast.

Yet from tears, a strength will rise,
Through the pain, we learn to cope.
Reflected in the endless skies,
We find the threads of fragile hope.

The Ribbons of Yesterday

Tied in knots, the past remains,
Memories worn, both sweet and sour.
Ribbons fall like gentle rains,
Weaving tales in every hour.

Time flows like a river wide,
Carrying whispers on the breeze.
In its grasp, we cannot hide,
Caught in moments, lost with ease.

Threads of laughter, strands of pain,
Entangled in the fabric's seams.
With every joy, comes the strain,
Life unfolds in haunting dreams.

Yet in each fold, a lesson learned,
In every tear, a glimmer bright.
From the ashes, hope is burned,
Into the shadows, we'll find light.

So we cherish the ribboned past,
In its warmth, we find our way.
For all those moments that won't last,
Shape the paths we walk today.

A Heart Shaped Void

In silence where love used to dwell,
An echo of laughter, a forgotten spell.
The shadows surround the empty space,
A heart shaped void, a timeless trace.

Memories linger like whispers of light,
Fading slowly into the night.
Each tear that falls, a story retold,
A heart once vibrant, now weary and cold.

Ghosts of the past dance in my mind,
Searching for warmth, but none can I find.
Each heartbeat echoes the love that was there,
Yet the silence remains, stretching everywhere.

Days turn to years in this hollowed out room,
Where shadows of joy now blossom in gloom.
I reach for the light that used to be true,
But find only darkness where once was you.

The void, once shallow, has grown so deep,
In the heart's recess, where memories weep.
A space once filled with laughter and love,
Now a heart shaped void, a sorrowful dove.

The Cracks in Time's Facade

Time wears a mask, cracked and frail,
Moments slip through like whispers and sail.
Each tick of the clock, a story undone,
Life's fleeting dance, a race never won.

In twilight, the shadows begin to blend,
Past and future, they twist and bend.
Faces forgotten, yet memories gleam,
Caught in the cracks of a long-faded dream.

Time stretches taut with a whispering sigh,
The stars blink softly, as if to deny.
Each tick a reminder of what we've lost,
In the cracks of time, we reckon the cost.

A tapestry woven of joy and despair,
Patterns of laughter and moments we share.
Yet the fabric shreds in its age-old embrace,
And hope is often a vanished trace.

In the silence, we search for the signs,
Through the cracks in time, a truth that aligns.
Our stories entwined in the fabric of fate,
As we navigate love with the hands of the late.

Wandering in the Aftermath

In the aftermath, I wander alone,
Searching for pieces that time has outgrown.
Lost in the dust of what used to be,
In the echo of footsteps that never found me.

The air is heavy, thick with regret,
Memories linger like whispers upset.
Each corner turned unveils another scar,
As I chase shadows, lost in the far.

The world spins on, indifferent and cold,
While I stand frozen in stories retold.
Hope flickers faintly like stars in the night,
Guiding the lost through their endless plight.

Yet amidst the ruins, a glimmer remains,
A spark in the dark where connection sustains.
Though wandering leads through paths fraught with pain,
In the human heart, love will rise once again.

So I gather the fragments, one piece at a time,
Repainting my canvas, a new form of rhyme.
Wandering boldly in the aftermath's call,
With love as my compass, I'll learn to stand tall.

The Spaces Where You Were

In every room, a shadow of you,
The warmth of your laughter, a melody true.
I trace the void where your presence once stayed,
In the corners of life, memories cascade.

The sofa whispers tales of our nights,
In the crackle of silence, our dreams take flight.
The spaces between us now stretch far and wide,
Yet I feel your essence, an unseen guide.

The kitchen lingers with echoes of meals,
Each bowl and each cup, a memory seals.
In the creak of the floor, I hear you still,
A reminder of warmth, a moment to fill.

Seasons have changed, yet the grief stays near,
In the spaces where you were, I shed every tear.
I plant seeds of love in the soil of despair,
Hoping to bloom in the light that you bear.

So I nurture the spaces, turning pain into grace,
As I hold on to laughter, a delicate trace.
In the heart's gentle cradle, I carry you near,
In the spaces where you were, you will always appear.

The Unseen Goodbye

In silence we part ways, soft and slow,
Words unspoken, though feelings flow.
A glance exchanged, a lingering sigh,
You walk away, my unseen goodbye.

Memories linger like shadows at dusk,
Whispers of moments, a bittersweet musk.
Holding on tight to a fleeting glance,
In the quiet night, we shared our dance.

Time rolls on, with each ticking beat,
The echo of laughter, both bitter and sweet.
Yet somewhere within, a warmth remains,
In the depths of hearts, love never wanes.

Underneath starlight, feelings still bloom,
In the darkened corners, there's space for gloom.
But light finds a way through the cracks in the wall,
A reminder of love that continues to call.

So here's to the moments that time cannot steal,
The unseen goodbye, the things that we feel.
Through every sunrise, a promise anew,
In the echoes of love, I will cherish you.

Echoes of Yesterday

In the hush of twilight, memories creep,
Whispers of laughter, secrets we keep.
Shadows dance gently, like ghosts in the night,
Echoes of yesterday, fading from sight.

Time flows like water, each moment a strand,
Weaving our stories, so silent, so grand.
Footsteps in silence, hopes intertwined,
Carvings of dreams from the ties that bind.

Sunset's warm glow wraps the world tight,
The past lingers softly, just out of sight.
We search for the echoes of what we once knew,
In the stillness of night, the heart beats true.

A gentle reminder that love will remain,
In the folds of our minds, joy mixed with pain.
As stars illuminate paths long since walked,
The echoes of yesterday softly talked.

Hold close the whispers that time has not claimed,
In the flickering shadows, our spirits are named.
Through each fleeting moment, in heartbeats we trust,
Echoes of yesterday in memories must.

Shadows in the Attic

Dust dances lightly in the dimming light,
Shadows in the attic fade into night.
Boxes of memories held with a sigh,
Forgotten whispers of time passing by.

Old photographs laughing, frozen in cheer,
Moments once cherished now distant and clear.
The creak of the floorboard, a story unfolds,
Tales of the young, the brave, and the bold.

Cobwebs like lace mark a threshold of dreams,
History lies waiting, or so it seems.
With every step closer, the heart starts to race,
Shadows in the attic, a familiar place.

Echoes of laughter now tangled in dust,
Each hidden treasure, a memory gust.
Time may have passed, but the spirit remains,
Locked in the shadows, like sun after rain.

So here in the quiet, I bow to the past,
For shadows and light, they forever will last.
In the attic of time, love's stories reside,
Whispering softly, where hearts confide.

Remnants of a Fading Dream

In the morning light, the dreams start to wane,
Gentle reminders of joy intertwined with pain.
Threads of a vision that danced through the night,
Now float like whispers, barely in sight.

Memories woven in shades of the past,
Fading like echoes that seldom last.
Once vibrant colors now muted and gray,
Remnants of a dream slowly drifting away.

Yet in that stillness, a flicker remains,
A spark of a hope, through losses and gains.
Though dreams may dissolve like mist in the air,
The essence of longing still lingers somewhere.

Through valleys of shadows, I search for a glimpse,
The essence of laughter, heart's jubilant chimps.
In fragments of joy, I gather the seams,
Holding each piece of my fading dreams.

So here in this moment, I capture the light,
For remnants of dreams are still shining bright.
In the tapestry woven of loss and of gain,
The heart's unyielding song will break through the rain.

The Burden of Leftover Wishes

In the silence, dreams reside,
Fading like whispers in the night.
Each hope a feather, gently laid,
On the scales of time, they light.

Moonlit paths, calling me near,
Yet the weight pulls back my heart.
Each wish remains, a quiet fear,
Torn between love and the part.

Yet I gather fragments of light,
With every step, shadows cast.
Weaving paths of wrong and right,
In the echoes of the past.

What we keep, what we let go,
A tapestry of our souls.
A burden of wishes, they grow,
Making us feel less than whole.

Still, the dawn will break anew,
With every sunrise, hope returns.
In each leftover dream, I'll sew,
A future built from what we yearn.

Shadows on the Horizon

In twilight's grasp, shadows play,
Dancing on the edges of light.
Whispers of dusk pave the way,
For dreams that linger, out of sight.

The horizon holds secrets dear,
Promises etched in amber hue.
Each step forward holds the fear,
Of what fades, yet of what is true.

With every breath, the day exhales,
Fading stars slip from our gaze.
In this dance, the heart prevails,
Chasing echoes through the maze.

Yet whispers call from far beyond,
Shadows stretching, reaching deep.
In the dusk, a quiet bond,
Awakens dreams within our sleep.

Embrace the night, let it guide,
The journey paved with silver light.
For shadows, too, are part of pride,
On the horizon, futures bright.

The Silhouettes That Fade

In the gloaming, silhouettes sway,
Ghosts of laughter fill the air.
Memories painted in shades of gray,
Whispering tales, moments rare.

With each passing hour, they blur,
Lost in the haze of distant stars.
Yet echoes of joy still occur,
Tracing the lines of who we are.

Like a candle, burning low,
Flickering dreams slip from my hand.
Yet in the dark, embers glow,
Mapping a future, unplanned.

As shadows stretch across the ground,
The past beckons, sweet and tight.
In silence, a lost sound,
Fades with the coming night.

But we dance in twilight's grace,
With hearts that beat, bold and brave.
Embracing the time and space,
For it's love that learns to save.

Reverberations of a Forgotten Home

In the stillness, echoes ring,
Memories linger, soft and low.
With every sigh, the heart will sing,
Of a time when love would flow.

The walls remember, whispers shared,
Laughter echoing through the halls.
In the shadows, moments bared,
Fallen leaves, like old, worn calls.

Yet now the silence carries weight,
Footsteps fade in dusty light.
Once a refuge, now it's fate,
A canvas painted with the night.

In corners, a forgotten tune,
Softly strumming on the air.
Each note, a ghost of afternoon,
Scattered dreams that linger there.

Home is where our hearts reside,
Though time may wear its gentle face.
Reverberations still abide,
In every tear, a warm embrace.

Milton Keynes UK
Ingram Content Group UK Ltd.
UKHW020042271124
451585UK00012B/999